I07563O3

FINISHING LINE PRESS
www.finishinglinepress.com

Humming Beneath the Mist

poems by

Abby Luby

Finishing Line Press
Georgetown, Kentucky

Humming Beneath the Mist

ISBN 979-8-89990-466-0 First Edition

ACKNOWLEDGMENTS

"Cherry Sigh" was published in the *Third Street Review*

"Fiddler's Grace Notes" and "Passion Plays" were published in *Syncopation Literary Journal*

"She Reaches Down Way-Seeking Past Memory's Lock" published in *Made From Midnight Anthology/PoetsInThePines*

Publisher: Leah Huete de Maines
Editor: Christen Kincaid
Cover Art: Hope Weissman
Author Photo: Michael Zucker
Cover Design: Elizabeth Maines McCleavy

Order online: www.finishinglinepress.com
also available on amazon.com

Author inquiries and mail orders:
Finishing Line Press
PO Box 1626
Georgetown, Kentucky 40324
USA

Contents

For my son Nick Belenko who, from infancy to adulthood,
has enhanced my perception of time
and
my dear family and close friends who have consistently
encouraged me to pursue creative writing.

"Art is the only way to run away without leaving home"
—Twyla Tharp

Cherry Sigh

He laughs in his sleep
as the cherry pie cools
on the rack

His somnolent smile coddles
the fruit in gelatinous languish
slip of syrup oozes
through a hole in the crust

Do the cherries recall
his knuckles nipping
their sinewy stems? Notching
out their pits? Shaping
the raw dough into
a sloped shallow bed
for toasty slumber?

Next to him, I dream of that stroll in Brooklyn
under the flushed light
of cherry blossoms his curved
palm over mine our veins aligned
warm flesh for my slim fingers
a squeeze baked in

Fiddler's Grace Notes

I swished around the womb
luxuriating as you played,
sonorous, resonate,
bow across the strings
that long, round note
and when I was born,
sound circled my tiny shell ears
melodies, crisp spiccato
from a meteor—
these, my childhood poems.
Your passion
your innate virtuosic charisma
each delicate grace note—
an angel's giggle
You love trying
different fiddles, in shops heady
with scents of sap-based rosin
and wood glue, gingerly play
a Strad, a moment.
Even at 94, violin under your chin—
hearing dulled
you rattle off cadenzas
pacing the floor, flashy
You always find the spot
on the D string with your middle finger,
the one smashed in a car door
when you were a kid
The bluntness of that
finger, stub with no nail,
radiating from your core
a lush vibrato.

Chanting the Universe Lopsided

Walking, turning the globe with your toes dug in,
not backing up. Keep your eye on the one cloud
that's always in the same place.

> Wait. Can you re-write that in a minor key
> while the violins evaporate on a high note?
> And—oh. Lean into the walking bass so it's more
> grounded.

Each step nudges the planet past its tilt,
an axis unnerved, bending fields of wild mustard,
ochres dancing with bees, sighing glissandos,
pollinator specs in the vast universe,
tiny filaments tittering in free fall.

> Hold on. Please re-shape the static cloud, floating
> off a faded painting in the dimmed gallery
> as critiques click off tangy tongues.

From outer space, among other dots
Our wobbly dot—in a stray of black holes
—could vanish all harmonies
While chanting the universe lopsided.

> Slow up. Kindly re-cast the air from dry to humid
> to soften the soil
> into a rich mud to better cradle your feet.

Sea Dragons

Leafy sea dragons reshape their limbs
as sea grasses, fooling piranha—
we camouflage to resist autocrats,
fooling the lawless bottom feeders.

We hear what we want to hear.
At the Philharmonic, flutes shift to brass,
we hear the key change. The running notes
fade between our ears.

We dread the grand finale, ending our
concert hall escape, safe from
O! the country is a slippery place,
our voices slide inaudible,
battered psyches quiver our gills.

We paddle up current, steadying
a non-persona backstroke, hover
above sea grasses, guarding our saturated limbs.

Passion Plays

Your heated gee-tar blues sizzle
my ears, prickles the flesh
your edgy steel strings groove
your fingers, a twang
strumming my innards

Do you know how
the blues soothe the back of the eyelids?

Your pursed lips angle
the high note, be-bop
capillaries in zing zang veins
pulses an off-kilter cake-walk to
deep thumps—
longing you can't see
under all those notes
music to undo myself.

She Reaches Down Way-Seeking Past Memory's Lock

her lover's tether fades as he leaves the earth fingers still tapping
notes on his violin, singing

curly vines   wa-wa vibrato   spilling   filling

inner lushy plucks like flutters—fish gills' last gasp.

His slack hand in hers, the waning off-beat pulse
like a stutter stuck on a syllable. Then, under blinking fluorescents

blue-gloved nurse banishes his ashen limp hands
into crusty, sanitized paper mittens
crack slap rip of Velcro, his sweet palms stolen.

Stops   med-tube yank-out & face scratching   says doc,
merciless & bolting from medical industrial sprawl, and here
are   futile   heart   pumps

She steps back as his trapped bony tendrils
flexes through decades of caresses, of tickling a warm baby's nose
fingers   that deftly   cracked eggs   with one hand
charming her for 60 years.

Shaft of Descent

I can't believe you're telling me
you don't love me, as we
go down in the elevator
        "*don't love*"—ricocheting
at sharp angles,
in the shaft of descent.

Outside, robotically, you take my hand.
Say you hold me
        "*in high regard*"—dissolving
intimacy, your chilled sentiment.

        Words—a scattering of particulates.

We used to be wrapped in the mere velocity
        of each other's voices
        words not important.
        Now, incoherent murmurs, a limp embrace.

Driving north you say,
        "*I'm just not feeling it.*"

Words, blasting a parabolic trajectory,
        slamming the macadam—fracturing.
        Syllables—crushed by speeding tires.

Still, I cling to your pauses,
random spaces between the stings.

        My diminishing sense of self.

On foot we look down
the valley, vast. The wind
propels us to our own jet streams.
                Your words, knotty gibberish—disintegrating.
                your features fade.

Flecks of squeezed light charge
into pin-pricking emptiness.

Ode to John Chamberlain

Inside the tangled metal the aorta
peeks out, magenta. She knows
her name among the random car parts,
screeching the scorched yellow cadmium,
a requiem's falsettos rippling
from within the crushed pile-up
still pulsating.

Note: This ekphrastic poem was inspired by John Chamberlain's "Slow Dancing to the News, "1981, one of his crushed metal car sculptures.

Bacon Strip Tease

Your heated sizzle
smoked slivers, crackling
molting & gurgling in your pool of lard,
less than you were,
like the shrinking promises of men,
briny ribbons swelling, like hope,
shedding oil from past lives,
reduced to an effable scrunch.

Saltiness flirts, teasing
a sugary thirst
for fruit's pulpy cool nectar,
pressed in a timeless sweep.

Where is the cool sweetened peach of eternity?

My Friend Bill

Months after the midnight call,
the nurse's heavy accent,
"No heartbeat, no vitals.
Come get the body."

What to keep? Pyramids of stuffed bears,
large ones grunting on the bottom,
small ones squeaking on top,
all dusty limp, all slumped over.
Shadows of your bear hugs. Our escapes into your cozy girth.
Boxes of vinyl records, CD's,
orphaned remotes, dead cell phones
still releasing your aura.
Lost computer passwords,
your data persona, levitating
in digital no man's land.
Water treatment manuals.
Maps of dams and waterways
shelved with your coveted erotica,
    dangling cocks, swelling bosoms
    seeking your gaze, then slipping off the page
to landfill oblivion. Detritus in free fall,
the dumpster's steely arms out
welcoming your large indented mattress, heaved,
    the top corner jutting to the sky,
your final unshackling.

You let go of who you were, shunning
your many illnesses like a bad plate of stew
    acidic, too salty.
Your clothes smell of cigarette smoke,
fried food, soy sauce,
    oddly endearing,
you craved sugary and tart,

Deep menthol inhales,
        the only pleasures left you said.
One beer left in the refrigerator,
        the one we might have shared
        our lips to the bottle, an alternating current
that lit our long friendship.

Scene 1: Restaurant Shoot

Dining room almost empty, patrons sated
        licking spoons, sipping sherry

Dolly-shot backwards, swerve to soapy hands, dirty plates
hot-steamed jets, scouring

        crumbs of faded dinner prattle

Jerky camera—wine glasses pinging, rinsed off

        lip stains mouthing chit chat

Pan to kitchen, exhaust fan whirs high

Cut to far end butcher block
        Chef's moving hulk, apron hiked up
        his salty penis between her lips
        (his vaporous chili breath) hot sauce sweat
        drips on her hair

Quick zoom—peppercorns embedded in her palms

Distant groans, door shuts

Close-ups
        Chef's buttery fingerprints on stove
        eggs simmering in pan, yolks still running.

Fall

You have to draw a line through the first memory, steer it to intersect with the next three flashbacks splitting the very soon future fear in half, that way the frontal capacity is energized, stinging almost, sliced by a bit of remorse. Oh, can't you feel the rush of seams splitting at the cusp of the moment? Just hold it, please, and sink to the bottom of the now, plant your feet in the fulcrum, pull down close but not touching the vortex, oblivious with your hand on my belly like a canopy shading a wide expanse of song in our heat, emerald leaves wriggling to our laughter, pressing into skin as summer fades into fall.

The Train

Lionel trains whiz around small steely tracks
a gray oval planted on green linoleum kitchen floor
my older brother, six, enthralled
Mom scrubs dishes steamy.

I kneel beside my brother, my knobby knees
too near the tracks
my knuckles press into the floor
I'm itching to push the controls,
the little red and blue levers he jerks up
and down, leaning in, spins
the train wheels faster.

Makes me think of summer
just me, Grandma, on the
Amtrak train to the big white beach
spongy feet in salt water.

She holds my hand, forests and fields blur
the train's chugga-chugga plays my veins
pulses my head heavy and floating
to her lumpy lap, a flowered skirt
moth ball infused petals slip into dreams, scatters
over miles of track.

I'm lost in those miles, like a small
fly dazzled by a loud giant worm that
makes my wiry hair-thin wings buzz,
pumping one sustaining drop of blood
a thread antenna steers my blip of a life
never growing up
like my wild-eyed brother, now frenzied
at the controls, hurtling the toy locomotive
screeching, lurching down the straight-away, rounds the curve—

my thumb on the tracks
jet streams of blood
Grandma lets go of my hand, a crushed wing

My thumb sticky wet
I crash to the floor, green-turning-black
dish clatter stops, Mother
upside down, shrieking my name
echoes from way down the tracks
I can't wait to feel the sand between my toes.

Lake Walking

Slip.

Lake frozen solid, crusty cold on my lips.
Why did he leave? Took his snowshoes.
Glassy black, ice fissures deep.

Can the fish see my feet?

Sorry about the child, he said—tough luck.
Frosted veins pulse our frozen divides.

Fish guys
Ruddy faces, chafed hands
Hunched over steely augers, spiraling blades
Crunch and gauging
the ice, a widening weak spot

Who's down there?

Bear down. There she came. The catch
reeled in long through the tunnel.
Deep warm dark became cold harsh light.
There was the head. Ten small breaths then push,
Was she breathing?

Catch them. Splay them. Gaspy gills.
Helpless fins. Small frozen shinnies
on the sheet in the sun. Eyes ice blank.

Stilled gelid tears. Frigid throat
frozen skin for gloves,
the lake moans a slow lament
crystallizing moisture in the air

Lake walking. Is it safe?
Cold clears the senses, freezes the heart
An opening iced over, hardened
Protected from future fishermen.

17 I.R.R., Paul Klee

Arrow darting black
the other adamant red
sweeping two faces off
the canvas

Hourglass eyes shimmy
with ire, an acerbic smirch

Her cunning curled ribbon lips
tease, citrus kisser
swan eyebrows
hover on the tilt

Cruising cachoogas
up-ley to turbulence
evaporating streamers
exit, yanked to a blank beyond.

Note:
"17 I.R.R." is an ekphrastic poem inspired by a Paul Klee painting "Siebzehn, irr" (1923), which translates to "Seventeen, Mad" or "Seventeen, Astray."

Java Press

Prickly brew
steeps beneath the
hovering press.

Stir first! I hiss—
No, you say firmly
the water teases
out the flavor, you can't

Impose yourself on nature
You can't interrupt
dark roast morsels embracing
water's douse.

the saxophone steam rises.

Stir! My spoon circles the air
I crave the crema swirl of
buff-colored froth,
aroma's halo.

You stay my wieldy spoon
a firm but gentle touch,
humming, press in hand.

Crunched beans afloat
as our moment simmers.

Buzzed

in a dustup of apples flinging
off branches,
sap filled pulp
tempts crows
squawking

the essence of the fruit tree
churns a sugary orbit
as black feathers splice the air
slip shod
the birds' honeyed shadows
tipsy, buzzed wings
the flock's groggy tumble
roiling into ragged crimson fruit skins
scattered seeds
sowed slow into earth's crust.

Morality Writhing

There's a snake on my roof
seeking to stop this poem, curling
over the eaves slow
diving down at my bedroom window.

Just as I see him this page slips
away towards the picture of my mother, long gone
her enigmatic smile.

These words I scrawl please her, a writer herself
inspired by great art depicting
serpents clutched by Eve, Cleopatra
coiling from Medusa's head, morality writhing
from canvas to canvas landing
on my roof, peering in my window
as the glass fades away.

The Undoing

It's time to stop our scrawled narrative zigzagging up the walls
seeking refuge and permanency in ceiling cracks.

We must shorten the dialogue
tone down the rhetoric
insert mild compassion, use
just   three   words.

Edit out sensual flashbacks
but let's not delete
'arching limbs'
'lips parting.'

Close the window on our future fantasies
take out frolics on the
oriental rug, whose stilled pile
is desire unwoven.

Draw blue velvet curtains, faded
shadows, tangled sheets
thrown off street clothes.

Change the arc of our characters
blur our features
drain the Jacuzzi, siphon away
our   floating   selves.

Put away the small secret gift
the white origami swan
use pursed lips for impact.

Finally undo. Yank the triste
from ceiling corners
tie off the ends at the door.

Ferrymen

We are a party
on a ferry, celebrating
Grandpa's birthday.

His cheeks flushed, silver hair askew
scarf loose around his neck
        his family together buoyant
        on the water.

In thrall of the river, the current grabs
our gaiety, flings our laughter
to the shore, clatter-slaps
against an old
silent smokestack, scorched
from decades of flames
        a candle blown out, a skein
        of white smoke curving up,
        a dissolving spine.

Our darling Grandpa teeters
        sees an eagle
        perched against the sky
        wings pressed against the wind sheer
eyes pierce beyond the currents
        scouring for glittering fins.

Through the bottom of his feet
        he feels the push of sharp crusted waves
        now on his toes, as if lifted by
jagged white caps jostling
skyward he is
pulled as if by translucent fishing lines
cast from astral planes
        by ageless ferrymen
cruising the churning waters.

Dystopian Rhapsody

Speeding down the skyway
on our floating mattress, slapping sheets
blacktop blurs, breezes
push our goosebumps.

We surge to the carnival fast lane
passing beds—springs creaking, screeching
couples slide sideways, some on trampolines,
others lumbering slipshod, twirling from bungie cords
negligees plaster moist skin.

Men grunting "oh god oh god," women
uttering interplanetary lingo.

A wind shear crack whacks
catapulting coitus, propels tangled limbs
in a Delphic sweep
to volcanic clouds.

Suddenly you and I swerve
off ramp, our bed careens
scrapes pavement, slithers through
an underpass
smothers our glow.

Then up-glide, a vista,
white hills glossed in blue light
our cushy platform hovers.

I fall off,
disheveled, quenched, tizzied
to the south side,
and you gone north.

Black Lives Have Always Mattered

Hidden cloaks. It could have been there were
no more white hoods in attics
in Nelsonville, New York. Stashed coarse linen, smoke-reeking,
clawed out from darkened rafters,
tossed and burned in oil drums in back yards.

It could have been that there were no more no photos
of hooded men at burials, Cold Spring cemetery, 1926.

We wish it never happened. Hudson Valley realtors
steering blacks away from neighborhoods,
You wouldn't be happy here,
to small back road cottages where it was safe
to pluck a soloed string stretched from a washtub,
to sing the blues.

There was a July day when men, women,
children were stoned as they swayed
to mighty Paul Robeson. Peekskill. 1949.
'I'm tired of livin'
But scared of dying.'

Cloaks reappear. Lethal underworld jabs
fan history, fade justice, sear the ether.
No more could have been. It is.

Not My Muse

The garish rabbit image
glares at me, angst off the canvas
harsh blue brush-jabs splatter
behind my retina,
an affront to the bloodstream.

You're no honky-tonk Modrian,
whose svelte moves, a heart beat
widens the brain space, tap tap tap

nope, not you. wielding a hare's anger
convulsing, provoking each brush stroke
a jump-scare emboldened

Your bumped-out splotches
hardly inspire me
I'm wagering you're not my muse.

not like Thelonious, his swift jazz riff
and deep pounding bass line
struts a winning gamble.

but what do I know?
inspiration stakes are high
I'm betting—without negative space,
your spiked rabbit blob ears
with no room for ambient sound
no   air   to   move   me

Flipping you upside down doesn't
endear your drab blues, doesn't
draw me to your stoney jowls

I'm betting
you're   not   my   muse
you didn't happen to me

Earthen Ware

for Anita

If there could be one last moment with her
just one before cancer's grasp
I would ask a go-back to the show of ceramic bowls.

How she marveled at the curves, imperfections
the rolled lips, her hands tingling with longing
for that glob of raw clay, pure, unblemished, pre-born.

Memory tapping her fingers, playing with the cool wet clay.
jaunty indents edge into funny shapes.

Her arms embracing the potter's wheel, tendrils of the spin
molding the egg-shaped bowl, wielding thickness to thin
thin to smooth, dissolving muddy tumors in a quiet twirl.

The kiln's fiery swelter rushes whistling air pockets
into a slow explosion of cells, the thrum of weakening veins
bowing to silent, slow dripping glazes.

The bowl blisters, bubbles, cracks, waves of hot air rise
while cool air falls, one form yields to another
a steady hardening that can never be reversed.

Years later this lone ceramic vessel holds an inner song
nurturing the single thumbprint on the bottom.

The Front Steps

The snake tightens around the neck of the poem,
curls the similes, spins verbs, shedding
skins of scratched-out lines, erases
darlings penned at night.

Squeezing disjointed typeface
she rasps the air,
molting margins crackle off the page,
hushed, she hugs the poem's slumped shoulders.

Rustling off refreshed
she settles on the front steps
waiting the poet's return.

The Stuff of Earth and Water

for Cynthia

The wind sang praise for ice sheets endless
saluted slow-shift glaciers crazy jagged
nudging oceans to largess.

Now, air struggles to blow away
earth's carbon-pressed cloak
choking every life zone.

Weather is an evil mixture of disorder
Ice caps tumble, dissolve
high tides froth skyward, crash slant
coast lines pummeled.

Unsuspended suns pound crusted lands

Raw, ear burning ignorance, proud oblivion
How to live, to learn, fold in resilience
We still chase green, seeding concrete
vines splay, crawl, lavish high towers
city trees down-steams the swelter, persist
Follow the cooling science.

Malcolm

Remember our pet spider monkey Malcolm?
walking the park, children gushed over him, his glassy eyes
pink face, his strong tail grip could hold on to anything
swishing the air.

He held our hands, the child we never had.

> *We tried.*
> *You: sex with lights on*
> *Me: eyes shut tight.*
> *You: upbeat salsa bop*
> *Me: crooning torch songs*
> *Where's our downbeat?*

Malcolm, unable to pull close our rigid hands.

We walked with Malcolm one last time
the kind zookeeper studied him.
Malcolm was a 'she,'—folks often mistook
the female's hanging labia for testicles.

They took him from us, our arms suddenly emptied
his reached towards us, a crude amputation.

We felt fooled not knowing Malcolm, our own selves.
we loved him/her anyway
not a big deal.

Your exit painful, dancing your funny two-step.
I saunter along in the park.

With Thanks

This little book would not have been possible without the guidance of poet and mentor extraordinaire DM Gordon, and lyric essay teacher Carla Carlson who taught at the Writing Institute at Sarah Lawrence.

Much appreciation for my cello teacher, Eliot Bailen, who has long kept my fingers connected to sound, nurturing my endless love of music.

To brilliant artist Hope Weissman who created this book's cover and to Mike Zucker whose expert eye snapped the perfect poet photograph.

And a special thanks to the wonderful folks at Finishing Press.

Abby Altman Luby grew up in the Bronx, New York City. Her father was a professional violinist who later became a lawyer, a state representative and then a judge. Although never published, her well-read mother was an avid writer who always shared her love of the written word with her three children.

Luby is an active cellist having earned a Bachelor of Arts degrees in Applied Cello and Journalism from Indiana University, Bloomington, IN. She graduated from the High School of Music and Art in New York City and with an Applied Music Certificate and Regents Diploma.

Her published short stories appear in *Parhelion* and *Persimmon Tree* and her poetry has been published in *Syncopation Literary Journal, Third Street Review,* and *Made From Midnight Anthology/ PoetsInThePines*. As a journalist she has reported for *The New York Daily News, SolveClimateNews, The Villager, The Real Deal, The Examiner News, Hook Magazine, Valley Table Magazine, Edible Hudson Valley.*

Humming Beneath the Mist is Luby's first published book of poetry.

http://abbyluby.com
https://www.facebook.com/abby.luby
https://x.com/abbyluby

www.ingramcontent.com/pod-product-compliance
Lightning Source LLC
LaVergne TN
LVHW090539110826
845146LV00003B/1182

* 9 7 9 8 8 9 9 9 0 4 6 6 0 *